Private Parts are (private)*

━━━━━━ ♥ ━━━━━━

*As you read, whenever you see the
word "(private),"
cup your hand around your mouth,
lean in close, and whisper it softly.

━━━━━━ ♥ ━━━━━━

Written by Kim Edmister
Illustrated by Tina Bozkurt

To my family—
For inspiring my passion to teach, guide, and protect.
The memories we create together are the
most treasured chapters of my life.

And with heartfelt appreciation
to those who advocate for children—
Your dedication makes the world
a safer, more hopeful place.

Note
to Parents & Educators

Dear Reader,

First, thank you for taking the time to read this book with a child. Tackling this topic isn't always easy, but it is incredibly important. Well—meaning parents, caregivers, and educators often feel unsure, uncomfortable, or unprepared to begin these conversations. But, the reality is that children need guidance and clear rules about body safety—early and often.

Private Parts Are Private is based on the lesson I shared with thousands of Pre—K—5 students during my 18 years as an elementary school counselor. It lays the foundation for ongoing conversations that give children the knowledge and confidence they need to help protect themselves from sexual abuse.

Why Start Early?

Some adults hesitate to introduce this sensitive topic, believing they should wait until a child is 'old enough.' However, 'old enough' may not be soon enough. By introducing these concepts early and reinforcing them as children grow, we normalize the topic and empower them to recognize unsafe situations, set boundaries, and seek help when needed.

Talking Points for a Meaningful Discussion:

- Your body belongs to you, and you have the right to protect it.
- No one is allowed to look at or touch your private parts unless there is a good reason.
- Talk about what might be considered 'good reasons' for someone to see or touch private parts—such as during a medical exam or when a young child needs help with bathing or wiping. Be sure to include any situations that reflect your family's values, routines, or cultural practices.
- Practice saying together: "NO! THAT'S PRIVATE!"
- Define "trusted adults" and help children identify the trusted adults in their lives.
- Rule #3: Pictures and videos of private parts are not allowed. This means no one (including YOU) is allowed to take pictures or videos of your private parts. It's also not okay to look at pictures or videos of other people's private parts.
- When discussing private parts safety rules, help children understand that these situations happen in real life to real children. Most of the time, the person who does this is someone the child knows, likes, and trusts—a family member, friend, neighbor, coach or club leader.
- When it does happen, children often feel scared, worried, and unsure of what to do. By talking together about safety rules and practicing what to do, they can feel more prepared and know how to respond.
- Older children may ask, "Why would someone do that?"—a difficult but common question. Consider responding in an age-appropriate, honest, and reassuring way. For example, you might explain that some people make bad choices, are confused about right and wrong, or try to trick children—but it is never the child's fault.
- Kids might worry about getting in trouble if they speak up. Explain that it takes courage to tell someone when something doesn't feel right. They will NOT be in trouble for sharing, and it's the adult's job to listen and help keep them safe.
- Stress that if one adult doesn't resolve the problem, they must keep speaking up—telling another and another until someone takes action. If a child feels embarrassed or afraid to speak up, encourage them to ask a friend for help. Sometimes, a friend may find it easier to approach an adult on their behalf.

A Final Thought for Caregivers

Many heartbreaking stories from survivors of childhood sexual abuse share a common thread: the abuse often occurs when children are in the care of others—at a sleepover, visiting a relative, or even at home when guests are present. Children rely on their caretakers to be vigilant about who has access to them and to remain committed to creating safe environments free from potential threats.

The reason we call them "private parts" is because (you say it with me) they're... (private).

There are four important safety rules for you to know about private parts.

You need to know the rules so that you can keep your private parts safe.

The four rules are...

SAFETY RULES FOR PRIVATE PARTS

1) No one is allowed to look at or touch your private parts, unless there is a good reason.

2) You are not allowed to look at or touch someone else's private parts.

3) Pictures and videos of private parts are not allowed.

4) Secrets about private parts are not allowed.

Did you know that there is ONLY ONE person who can look at or touch your private parts any time they want?
(Can you guess who?)

It's perfectly fine when small children need help washing or wiping private parts until they learn how to do it for themselves.

Getting help with washing or wiping is a good reason for someone else to see or touch your private parts.

Just like there are times when your stomach, ear or throat hurts, private parts can sometimes hurt. When private parts are hurting (no matter the reason) a trusted adult can help.

When you go for a check-up with a trusted adult, the doctor will look at and touch different parts of your body to make sure you're healthy.
A check-up is another time when it's okay for someone, like a doctor, to look at or touch your private parts.

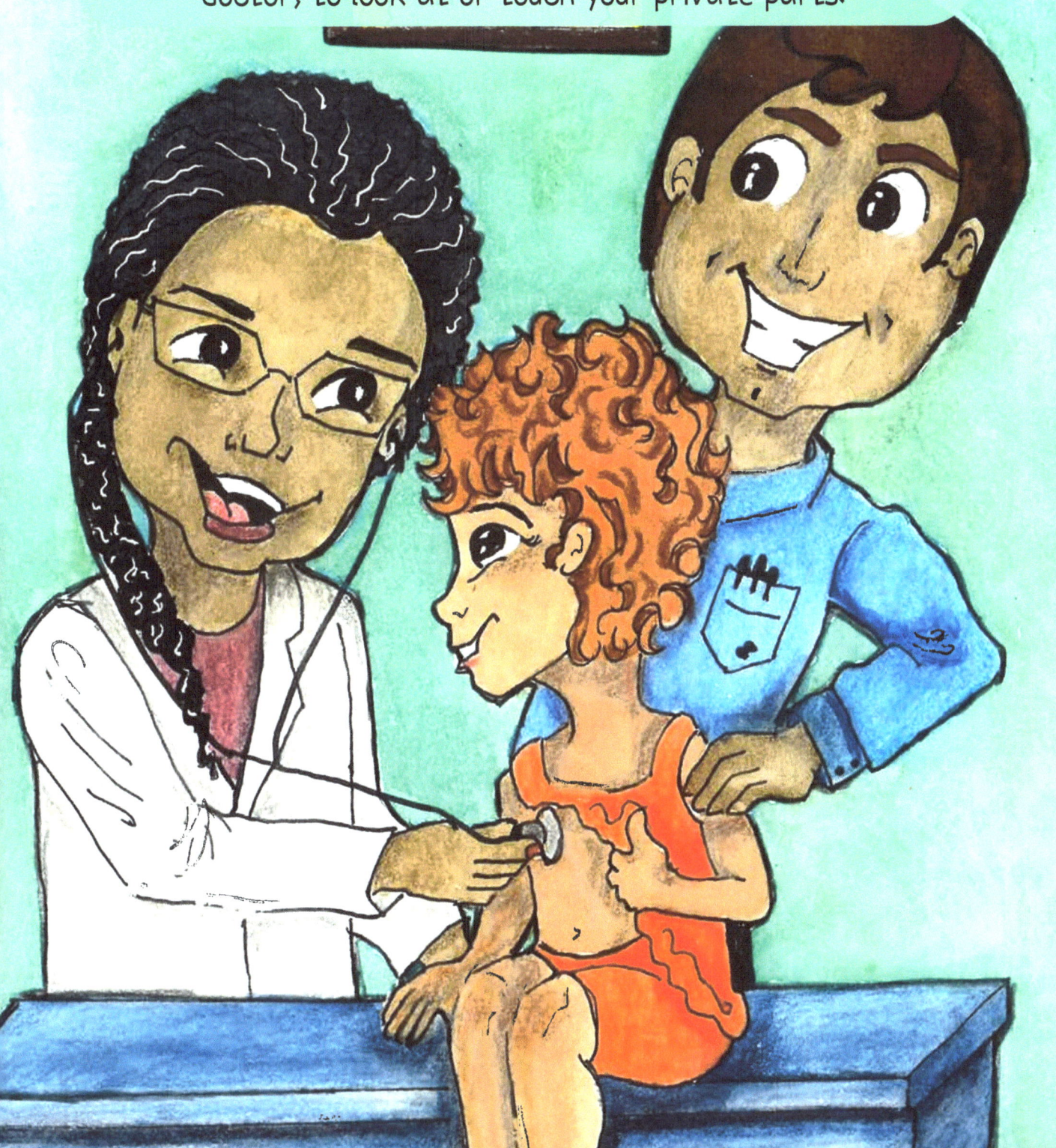

At home, you might sometimes see someone naked.
That's perfectly fine,
unless it makes you feel uncomfortable.

If someone wants to take pictures or videos of your private parts, you can make an angry face and say in your meanest, loudest voice, "NO! THAT'S PRIVATE!" Then, run and tell a trusted adult right away! Let's practice that again together. Ready? "NO! THAT'S PRIVATE!"

Secrets about private parts are not allowed. If someone asks you to keep a secret about private parts, your job is to tell a trusted adult right away.

Kids are never EVER in trouble when they ask for help to keep their private parts safe.
If you don't get the help you need the first time you ask, tell a different adult (and keep telling!)...until you do.

GO! GO!

SAFETY RULES FOR PRIVATE PARTS

1) No one is allowed to look at or touch your private parts, unless there is a good reason.

2) You are not allowed to look at or touch someone else's private parts.

3) Pictures and videos of private parts are not allowed.

4) Secrets about private parts are not allowed.

Knowing and following the safety rules for private parts helps to keep kids healthy and safe!

Who are the trusted adults that help keep YOU safe?

SAFETY RULES FOR PRIVATE PARTS

1) No one is allowed to look at or touch your private parts, unless there is a good reason.

2) You are not allowed to look at or touch someone else's private parts.

3) Pictures and videos of private parts are not allowed.

4) Secrets about private parts are not allowed.

Private Parts are (private)

Written by Kim Edmister
Illustrated by Tina Bozkurt

www.ingramcontent.com/pod-product-compliance
Lightning Source LLC
Chambersburg PA
CBHW041604120626
46551CB00002B/307